Dwyane Wade

Jeff C. Young

Mason Crest Publishers

Produced by OTTN Publishing in association with
21st Century Publishing and Communications, Inc.

MASON CREST PUBLISHERS INC.
370 Reed Road
Broomall, Pennsylvania 19008
(866) MCP-BOOK (toll free)
www.masoncrest.com

Printed in the United States of America.

First Printing

9 8 7 6 5 4 3 2 1

Library of Congress Cataloging-in-Publication Data

Young, Jeff C., 1948-
   Dwyane Wade / Jeff C. Young.
     p. cm. — (Modern role models)
   Includes bibliographical references.
ISBN 978-1-4222-0492-4 (hardcover) — ISBN 978-1-4222-0779-6 (pbk.)
   1. Wade, Dwyane, 1982–   —Juvenile literature. 2. Basketball players—United
States—Biography—Juvenile literature. I. Title.
GV884.W23Y68 2008
796.323092—dc22
[B]   2008033042

Publisher's note:
All quotations in this book come from original sources, and contain the spelling
and grammatical inconsistencies of the original text.

CROSS-CURRENTS

*In the ebb and flow of the currents of life we are each influenced
by many people, places, and events that we directly experience
or have learned about. Throughout the chapters of this book you
will come across CROSS-CURRENTS reference boxes. These
boxes direct you to a CROSS-CURRENTS section in the back
of the book that contains fascinating and informative sidebars
and related pictures. Go on.* ▸▸

CONTENTS

Miami Heat guard Dwyane Wade holds up his trophy as NBA Finals MVP, June 20, 2006. The Heat had just defeated the Dallas Mavericks, 95-92, to win Game Six and secure the NBA title. Dwyane's play throughout the series was outstanding, and he dropped 36 points in the championship-clinching game.

1

2006 Finals MVP

IN 2006, THE MIAMI HEAT ADVANCED TO THE championship round of the National Basketball Association (NBA) playoffs for the first time in their 18-year history. After the first two games of the best-of-seven series, however, it looked as though the Heat would not be around for long. The Dallas Mavericks had won those games on their home court.

In the first two games of the series, Dallas had used a simple but effective strategy—keep Miami's star center Shaquille O'Neal from taking shots. The Mavs would **double-team** and sometimes **triple-team** Shaq. That forced Shaq to pass rather than shoot. When Shaq did try to score, the Mavs intentionally fouled him, knowing that the big center was a poor free-throw shooter. In Game One, Shaq was just 1-for-9 from the foul line as the Mavericks won, 90-80. Game Two was even worse. Shaq took only five shots and missed six of his seven free throws as the Mavs won again, 99-85.

In the first two games, Miami's young star Dwyane Wade had tried to pick up the slack for Shaq. Wade scored 51 points and grabbed 14 rebounds in the two losses. Those were impressive stats, but if Miami was going to avoid a sweep, Dwyane would have to do even better in the upcoming contests.

CROSS-CURRENTS

Miami was a relatively new team when it first played for the NBA title. For the team's history, see "NBA Expansion." Go to page 46. ▶▶

⤜ THIRD-GAME TURNAROUND ⤛

Miami fans hoped that a return to their home court at American Airlines Arena would turn things around. The Heat got off to a good start in Game Three. After one quarter, Miami led 29-21, and at halftime the Heat were up 52-43.

Then, in the third quarter, Miami lost its momentum. Dallas outscored them, 34-16, to take a 77-68 lead. The once noisy Heat fans were now silent. With just one 12-minute quarter remaining to play, it seemed that Dallas was about to take a three-games-to-none lead in the series.

Things grew worse for the Miami fans. With 6:34 left on the clock, Dallas was in control of the game, holding a 13-point lead. Dwyane did not get frustrated or anxious, however. Instead, he would later tell *Sports Illustrated*, he knew his team was still capable of winning the game:

❝Thirteen points down with six minutes to go? That's not life or death. I've been through more than anybody knows. To me this is joy. This is when I can let it all out. This is my time. ❞

Dwyane took over, scoring 15 points in the final quarter as the Heat came back to take the lead. In the last few minutes, Miami forced the Mavericks to make five turnovers and miss five of seven shots. With just over three seconds left, and the Heat clinging to a one-point lead, Dwyane grabbed a crucial rebound and was fouled. He made one of his foul shots, and the Heat escaped with a 98-96 win. Dwyane finished as the game's leading scorer with 42 points, and also led in rebounds with 14.

⤜ ROAD TO VICTORY ⤛

Dwyane's clutch performance in Game Three was a preview of what he'd do in the rest of the championship series. Despite playing with

Dwyane Wade and Miami teammate Alonzo Mourning battle Dallas Mavericks center Erick Dampler for a rebound in action from Game Two of the 2006 NBA Finals. Dallas held Miami big man Shaquille O'Neal to just five points to win the game, 99-85.

a sore knee, Dwyane lit up the court with a 36-point, six-rebound performance in Game Four. With Dwyane running wild, the Mavericks could no longer gang up on Shaq. Freed from the heavy coverage, O'Neal added 17 points and 13 rebounds as Miami scored a surprisingly easy 98-74 win. Afterward, Dwyane said that for the first time in the championship series, he was back to playing the way he felt he should:

"I'm just in rhythm. I'm a rhythm player. The first two games in Dallas, I was kind of off my rhythm and now I'm in a rhythm. I'm able to look and see the defense come before it's coming and make my moves, pull up or attack."

Game Five was the closest game of the series. Once again, Dwyane came through when it mattered the most. With nine seconds left in

Miami Heat coach Pat Riley and his team celebrate the franchise's first-ever NBA title by raising the Larry O'Brien NBA Championship Trophy, June 20, 2006. Dallas had won the first two games of the series, only to see Miami roar back to take four straight, including the clincher on the Mavs' home court.

overtime and his team losing by a point, he dribbled his way through four Dallas defenders before being fouled by Dirk Nowitzki. With the game on the line, Dwyane coolly sank two free throws to give the Heat a 101-100 win. He finished with a game-high 43 points.

⟫ NBA CHAMPIONS ⟪

When the Heat traveled back to Dallas for Game Six, Miami's coach, Pat Riley, packed only one suit. He was confident that the Heat wouldn't need two games to wrap up the championship series. He was right. Dwyane's 36 points and 10 rebounds helped give the Heat a 95-92 win—and their first NBA title.

Afterward, Dallas coach Avery Johnson admitted that no matter what the Mavericks tried to do on defense, Dwyane couldn't be stopped:

> **❝We tried a lot of things, but he just had a lot of desire to get it done. . . . Some of that stuff you just can't teach. When a player is making those kinds of plays, it's really no tricky play. He's beating double-teams, he's beating triple-teams. There's no tricks here.❞**

Dwyane's average of 34.7 points and 7.8 rebounds a game in the 2006 NBA Finals made him an overwhelming choice as the series Most Valuable Player. But when he stood at center court after Game Six to receive the MVP trophy, he modestly reminded everyone that basketball is a team sport:

> **❝This is a team award, just like it's a team championship. Man, it's one of the best feelings, next to my wife and my son, it's one of the best feelings I've ever had in my life.❞**

CROSS-CURRENTS

To learn about other great players who have been named Most Valuable Player in the NBA Finals, see "NBA Finals MVPs." Go to page 47. ▶▶

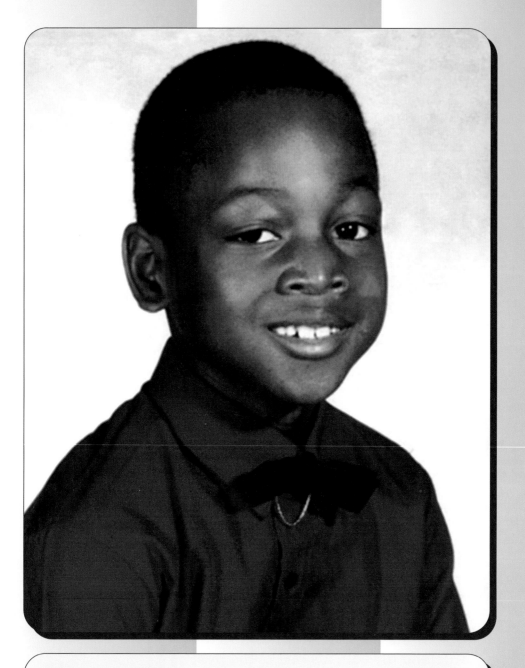

Dwyane spent much of his childhood in a poor neighbor-hood on the South Side of Chicago, where he lived with his mother and older sister. At age eight, however, his mother sent Dwyane to live with his father's family. After the family moved to the Chicago suburb of Robbins about a year later, Dwyane got his introduction to basketball.

A Hard Beginning

DWYANE WADE WAS BORN IN 1982 INTO A troubled home. His father, Dwyane Wade Sr., and his mother, Jolinda Wade, were both involved with drugs. They split up when Dwyane was still an infant. As a young child, Dwyane lived with his mother and older sister in a poor neighborhood on the South Side of Chicago.

Unfortunately, Jolinda eventually started dating a man who was abusive. She protected Dwyane by sending the eight-year-old away to live with his father. Dwyane's older sister Tragil packed a few clothes for him, then took him on the 15-minute bus ride to his father's house.

⇒ A NEW HOME ⇐

Dwyane moved into a crowded home. Dwyane Sr. was engaged to a woman who had three children of her own. About a year after Dwyane moved in, his father's family moved to Robbins, a small suburban town outside of Chicago. The new house had a garage with a well-worn basketball hoop attached to a wooden backboard. That's where Dwyane learned how to play basketball.

CROSS-CURRENTS

To learn about one of Dwyane's favorite players when he was growing up, check out "Dwyane's Role Model: Michael Jordan." Go to page 48. ▶▶

Wade family basketball games started early in the morning, broke for school, then resumed and continued until late at night. Dwyane, his father, and two of Dwyane's stepbrothers played hard. Fouls were never called. Points were usually scored by attacking the basket. Players who shot jumpers were accused of being afraid to drive for the hoop.

Dwyane Sr. showed his kids no mercy. He'd throw a hip or shoulder to knock them off-balance as they shot. That taught Dwyane how to shoot the leaners and running shots he uses today. No matter how many times Dwyane hit the ground, he'd always bounce back and attack the basket again. He later said,

> **❝[My father] taught me the game, what I needed to know to win games. My toughness on the court came from him knocking me down and not picking me up. ❞**

While Dwyane was honing his basketball skills, his mother's drug problems continued. In September 1992, Jolinda was arrested for possessing crack cocaine and sentenced to 14 months' probation. When Jolinda was caught selling crack while on probation, she was arrested again and sent to prison.

Dwyane visited his mother in jail once. This was a painful experience for the young man. He later called this period the worst time of his life.

⇒ HIGH SCHOOL ⇐

At H. L. Richards High School in Oak Park, Illinois, Dwyane played both football and basketball. As a sophomore, he didn't start or get much playing time with the basketball team. During the summer before his junior year, however, Dwyane grew four inches. This growth spurt led him to focus on basketball, and he worked hard on his shooting and ball handling. One of Richards High's basketball coaches gave Dwyane some vital one-on-one coaching. Dwyane made the varsity team in his junior year and quickly became one of the team's leaders offensively and defensively.

Before Dwyane's senior year, he moved in with the family of his girlfriend, Siohvaughn Funches, because of problems at home. That year, he led the Richards Bulldogs to a 24-5 record. In the state tournament, the Bulldogs advanced to the AA sectional finals before they were eliminated.

Although Dwyane had averaged more than 25 points and 10 rebounds a game during his senior year, his test scores were not as impressive. Dwyane's performance on the American College Testing

Dwyane played basketball and football at H. L. Richards High School in Oak Park, Illinois. But it wasn't until his junior year—after he had experienced a growth spurt— that Dwyane became a star. During his senior season, Dwyane averaged more than 25 points and 10 rebounds per game.

Playing for Marquette University's basketball team, Dwyane dunks in a game against Louisville. After sitting out his first year because he was academically ineligible, Dwyane exploded onto the college basketball scene during the 2001–02 season. He led Marquette in scoring, rebounding, assists, blocked shots, and steals and garnered an Honorable Mention for the Associated Press All-American team.

(ACT) college-entrance exam made most colleges reluctant to offer him a scholarship. Only three NCAA Division I schools—DePaul University in Chicago, Illinois State in Normal, and Marquette University in Milwaukee—actively recruited him.

Dwyane chose Marquette. Because of his low ACT scores, however, he was not allowed to play basketball during his freshman year.

⟫ COLLEGE CAREER ⟪

At the end of his first year at Marquette, Dwyane had a solid B average. This made him eligible to play during the 2001–02 season. He quickly established himself as the team's star player by leading the Golden Eagles in scoring, rebounding, blocked shots, steals, and assists. Marquette's 26-7 record got them into the NCAA Tournament, but they lost in the opening round.

After only one year, Dwyane was recognized as one the best players in his conference and one of the better young players in the country. He made the All-Conference USA first team and received Honorable Mention for the Associated Press All-American team.

Marquette fans expected Dwyane to take the team much farther in 2002–03, and he did. With Dwyane as the Golden Eagles' leading scorer and shot blocker, Marquette posted a 27-6 record and easily qualified for the NCAA Tournament. Marquette advanced to the Final Four by knocking off Kentucky, one of the tourney's top seeds. Dwyane posted a **triple-double** by scoring 29 points, grabbing 11 rebounds, and dishing out 11 assists.

Although Marquette was defeated in the Final Four by Kansas, the team's success brought

> **CROSS-CURRENTS**
>
> Read "History of the NCAA Tournament" to learn more about the biggest event for college basketball players.
> Go to page 49. ▶▶

Dwyane a batch of new honors and awards. The Associated Press named him a First Team All-American. Conference USA honored Dwyane by voting him its Best Defensive Player and the Conference Player of the Year. Dwyane's outstanding play was also attracting the attention of NBA teams and scouts.

Dwyane had other priorities besides basketball and school, however. He had married Siohvaughn in 2002, the year their first child, Zaire, was born. With a wife and a son to support, Dwyane decided to skip his final year of college. In May 2003, he announced that he was leaving Marquette to enter the NBA draft.

DRAFT PICK #5

2003 **topps** ROOKIE CARD 2004

DWYANE WADE

Dwyane Wade's rookie card. In the 2003 NBA draft, Dwyane was chosen fifth overall by the Miami Heat. Some basketball experts consider the 2003 draft class the most talented ever. The four players picked ahead of Dwyane were, in order, LeBron James, Darko Milicic, Carmelo Anthony, and Chris Bosh.

3

A Rookie Makes an Impact

BECAUSE OF HIS IMPRESSIVE COLLEGE CAREER, Dwyane Wade was expected to be a first-round selection in the 2003 NBA draft. Experts were unsure where he would be picked, however. *Sports Illustrated,* for example, predicted that Dwyane would be the ninth player chosen. Dwyane was actually the fifth player selected that year.

Some people criticized the Miami Heat's decision to take Dwyane. These experts believed the Heat needed a big man to play center, not a 6-foot-4 guard. Miami officials never wavered from their choice, however. The Heat quickly signed Dwyane to a three-year contract that paid slightly over $7 million. Dwyane wondered how getting so much money would change his life:

CROSS-CURRENTS

For more background on the players drafted along with Dwyane, check out "The 2003 NBA Draft." Go to page 50. ▶▶

"God has blessed me with so many earthly things. It seemed so dark for 21 years, and then I've come into this newfound money and life and excitement. It's scary because once you get to the point where you're so high? There's nowhere else for you to go but down. Will I fall? How hard is that fall going to be? What is going to come with that fall?**"**

⇛ SLOW START ⇚

Dwyane was in the starting lineup when the Heat opened their 2003–04 season against the Philadelphia 76ers. In his first regular season game, he led the Heat in scoring with 18 points. Still, the Heat lost, 89-74, and they proceeded to get off to a terrible start. Miami lost its first seven games. By early December, the Heat had a 5-15 record and their fans weren't seeing much improvement from the 2002–03 team that finished last in the Atlantic Division.

By mid-December the Heat began turning things around just as Dwyane was leading the team in scoring for six straight games. Miami won four of those six, and Dwyane scored 151 points in that span to average 25.2 points per game. In early January, however, a bone bruise on Dwyane's right wrist sidelined him for 13 games.

Without Dwyane, the Heat went 6-7 and their record dropped to 19-26. The season was about halfway over, and they were seven games under .500. It didn't look as if the Heat had much chance to make the playoffs.

In late February, Dwyane was named the Eastern Conference's Player of the Week. He became the first Heat rookie to win that honor. Even after he returned to the starting lineup, however, the Heat kept losing more than they were winning. On March 2, they were still only 25-36.

Miami finished the season strong, however, winning 17 of its last 21 games. That put the Heat into the playoffs with a 42-40 record. In spite of missing 21 games due to injuries, Dwyane put up some really impressive numbers in his rookie season. He averaged 16.2 points, 4.0 rebounds, and 4.5 assists per game. He was a unanimous choice for the NBA's 2004 All-Rookie Team, and he was third in the Rookie of the Year voting behind two of the most outstanding rookies in recent years, LeBron James and Carmelo Anthony.

Manu Ginobili of the San Antonio Spurs tries to draw a charge as Dwyane Wade rises over him for a layup, December 14, 2003. During his rookie season, Dwyane lived up to the Heat's expectations. He averaged more than 16 points per game and finished third in Rookie of the Year balloting, behind only LeBron James and Carmelo Anthony.

⇒ Becoming a Leader ⇐

As Dwyane showed steady improvement in his rookie season, even his veteran teammates began looking up to him as a team leader. Teammate Brian Grant noted that the Heat were now running plays to get the ball to him. Dwyane's style of cutting and slashing his way to the hoop was getting him more shots.

Dwyane was enjoying his new role as a player who made things happen on both ends of the court. He told *Sports Illustrated*:

> **"At the beginning of the year I was hoping to contribute and feed off of my teammates. Now it's reversed, and the guys are feeding off of me."**

⇒ Playoffs—New Orleans ⇐

Miami faced the New Orleans Hornets in the first round of the playoffs. It was the Heat's first playoff appearance in three years. In Game One, Dwyane showed everyone that he could be the go-to guy when the game was on the line. With 1.3 seconds left, he hit a running jumper to give Miami an 81-79 win.

Dwyane finished Game One with a game-high 21 points along with five rebounds and five assists. The 21 points he scored were the most by a Heat rookie in a playoff game. His premiere playoff game showed everyone that the postseason playoffs were going to be an extension of an already outstanding rookie season.

In Game Two, Dwyane's team-high six assists helped lead the Heat to a 93-63 blowout win. Dwyane had his worst playoff performance in Game Three. He was held to just two points while missing seven of eight shots. He came back strong in Game Four, however, with **double-double** stats of 11 points and a team-high 10 assists. Still, the Heat lost to New Orleans, 96-85.

Game Five saw Dwyane making another clutch basket late in the game. With 54.4 seconds left, he hit a three-point shot to break an 80-80 tie. The Heat went on to win the game, 87-83. The Hornets took Game Six, 89-83, despite Dwyane's game-high 27 points. The Heat came back from this disappointing loss, however, with an 85-77 win in Game Seven to advance to the next round of the playoffs, the conference semifinals. Dwayne helped ensure the win in that crucial series-deciding game by scoring 12 points and getting 7 assists.

Before a packed house at Miami's American Airlines Arena, Dwyane Wade celebrates his game-winning shot in overtime, November 19, 2004. The jumper lifted the Heat over the Utah Jazz, 107-105. That day, Dwyane led all scorers with 39 points. He also dished a game-high eight assists and picked up three steals and a pair of blocked shots.

≫ PLAYOFFS—INDIANA ≪

In the Eastern Conference Semifinals, Miami faced the Indiana Pacers. Dwyane continued to enjoy an outstanding playoff series against Indiana. In four of the six games, he was the Heat's leading scorer. He also posted a double-double in Game Five with 16 points and 10 assists. And yet, that wasn't enough to prevent the Pacers from taking the series, four games to two.

By anyone's standards, Dwyane had a truly outstanding post-season performance. He started in all 13 of Miami's playoff games and averaged 18.0 points, 5.6 assists, and 4.0 rebounds a game. He also became the only rookie in the history of the Heat to lead the team in scoring average in the postseason.

⋙ HIGH PRAISE ⋘

Even though he had finished third in the Rookie of the Year voting, some sportswriters believed Dwyane's progress surpassed that of all other rookies. One was *Sports Illustrated* writer Ian Thomsen, who had this to say:

> **❝No rookie, including LeBron James and Carmelo Anthony, has improved more rapidly than Wade, 22, who wondered if he was athletic enough to beat NBA defenders off the dribble when he turned pro . . . Wade has learned how to recognize defenses and initiate the Heat's new motion offense.❞**

⋙ 2004 OLYMPICS ⋘

After the playoffs ended for the Heat, Dwyane didn't get much time to rest. He was chosen to play for the United States in the 2004 Olympics in Athens, Greece. The United States had expected to have a roster full of experienced NBA stars on its team. For one reason or another, however, many of the biggest NBA stars chosen for the team avoided the Olympics. Kobe Bryant, Ray Allen, Jason Kidd, Kevin Garnett, and Tracy McGrady all skipped the Olympics after being picked for the U.S. team. The team was still left with some experienced NBA players like Stephon Marbury and Allen Iverson, but three major players on the team—Dwyane, LeBron James, and Carmelo Anthony—only had one year of pro experience apiece.

Playing for the U.S. team, Dwyane averaged 7.3 points and 2.4 assists per game. Many people thought Dwyane looked too hesitant to shoot the ball. They also noted that his field goal shooting percentage was a lowly 38 percent. Some blamed the low percentage on Dwyane being forced to play the **point guard** position during the Olympics. Allen Iverson became the **shooting guard** for the U.S. team and therefore had more chances to score.

The U.S. team took home the bronze medal for finishing in third place. For most U.S. fans, that was a big disappointment. The United States had won the gold medal in every Olympics since 1992—the year of the "Dream Team"—when NBA players were first permitted to play in the Olympics.

Dwyane was also disappointed with the performance of the U.S. team, but he thought it was unfair of fans and commentators to criticize the NBA players who had given up their short off-season to play for the United States. He told a writer from *The Sporting News*,

CROSS-CURRENTS

To learn more about the experiences of previous American Olympic basketball teams, read "U.S. Teams in Olympic Basketball." Go to page 51. ▶▶

During the medals ceremony for men's basketball at the 2004 Summer Olympics in Athens, Greece, disappointment is written on the faces of members of the U.S. team. The Americans had managed only a bronze medal. From left: Emeka Okafor, LeBron James, Carmelo Anthony, Carlos Boozer, Dwyane Wade.

DWYANE WADE

Shaquille O'Neal puts on a display of dunking power while Dwyane Wade observes. The occasion is a basketball camp for youth held in Miami and sponsored by Nestlé Crunch. Before the start of the 2004–05 NBA season, the Miami Heat traded for O'Neal, one of the most dominant big men in the game.

66 I wasn't excited to get the bronze. I wanted the gold. But to hear everyone talk about it like it was our fault, when we were the ones who gave up our summers to go over there and represent our country, that was not fair. 99

⇒ BIG TRADE FOR A BIG MAN ⇐

Before the start of the 2004–05 season, the Heat made a blockbuster trade by acquiring Shaquille O'Neal from the Los Angeles Lakers. They gave up a lot to bring Shaq to Miami. The Heat traded away three players—Caron Butler, Brian Grant, and Lamar Odom—who had been starters. On top of that, they also gave the Lakers their first-round pick in the 2004 draft. But Heat president Pat Riley believed that having a dominating big man was the key to winning an NBA title. From 2000 to 2002, Shaq had helped lead the Lakers to three straight NBA championships while winning the NBA's Finals MVP Award all three years.

Many sportswriters and NBA fans were predicting that the Heat would become a vastly improved team. Some of them expected Miami to strongly contend for an NBA championship. Dwyane was really excited about having Shaq as a teammate. He looked forward to a season in which the Heat could go deeper into the playoffs.

Pat Riley made it known that he thought Shaq would help lead the Heat to an NBA championship. Here is what he had to say to *Basketball Digest* about landing the big guy:

66 From junior high on up to the pros, in every single game where I played for a championship, either I was beat because the other team had the big guy or I won because we had the big guy. . . . I know how important the dominant big man is in the game of basketball. 99

Dwayne Wade may have become an NBA superstar as well as a crossover celebrity—*People* magazine named him to its list of the "50 Most Beautiful People" in 2005—yet he remained humble and unassuming. "Dwyane knows who he is," Tom Crean, his college coach, remarked. "He's in a situation where people want to make him superhuman. He doesn't see himself that way."

Steady Improvement

AT THE START OF THE 2004–05 SEASON, A CALF injury limited Shaq's playing time. Yet, the big center still had an immediate impact on the team. The double-teams that Shaq drew made it easier for Dwyane to get good shots. Instead of having to take jumpers, Dwyane could attack the basket. Miami started the season with four straight wins.

By mid-January Dwyane was averaging over 23 points, 5 rebounds, and 7 assists per game. The addition of Shaq was making Dwyane an even better and more productive player. Many fans and sportswriters were saying that Dwyane had become the Heat's most valuable player. One of these was *Sports Illustrated*'s Jack McCallum, who wrote:

> **"**Believe it. The emergence of Wade, more than the arrival of O'Neal, has been the **catalyst** for the vastly improved Heat. . . . [It] is Wade's combination

of abundant skill and **precocious** will that has carried Miami. ⁹⁹

⇒ ROLLING ALONG ⇐

As Shaq's playing time and Dwyane's scoring, rebounding, and assist numbers increased, the Heat continued to improve. In December 2004, Miami set a club record by winning 14 games in a row. Then, in late February and early March, the Heat put together a 12-game winning streak. Twice that season, their coach, Stan Van Gundy, was named NBA's Coach of the Month. The Heat easily won the Southeast Division of the Eastern Conference with a 59-23 record.

CROSS-CURRENTS

To learn more about Shaq, the NBA superstar who joined Dwyane's team in a 2004 trade, read "Shaquille O'Neal." Go to page 52. ▶▶

In the opening round of the playoffs, the Heat swept the New Jersey Nets in four games. Dwyane averaged 27.8 points and 8.8 assists per game during the series. But as outstanding as he was in the opening round, he would get even better in the Eastern Conference Semifinals against the Washington Wizards. After the Heat won Game One against Washington, 105-86, Dwyane set three team playoff records in Game Two by scoring 31 points, dishing 15 assists, and shooting 19 free throws. Sportswriter Eric Reid described his performance in glowing terms:

⁶⁶Wade controlled the game in a manner so complete that it was awe-inspiring and historic. It just may have been the greatest effort in Miami's 70 game playoff history. . . . Dwyane Wade is carrying the team right now. There is no hotter player at the moment in these playoffs than him. ⁹⁹

⇒ ANOTHER SWEEP ⇐

Game Three had Dwyane turning in another 31-point performance along with 9 rebounds, 6 assists, and 2 blocked shots. That put the Heat up 3-0 and gave them seven straight playoff wins.

In Game Four, it looked as if the Wizards might get their first win against the Heat. Washington led at the half, 51-47, but in the second half, Dwyane once again took control of the game. He scored 26 points in the final two periods and finished with 42 points to give Miami a 99-95 win.

Dwyane soars past 7'6" Yao Ming of the Houston Rockets during a January 5, 2005, game at American Airlines Arena in Miami. The Heat won the game, 104-95. In 2004–05, with Dwyane and Shaquille O'Neal powering the offense, Miami notched 59 wins during the regular season, the highest total in franchise history.

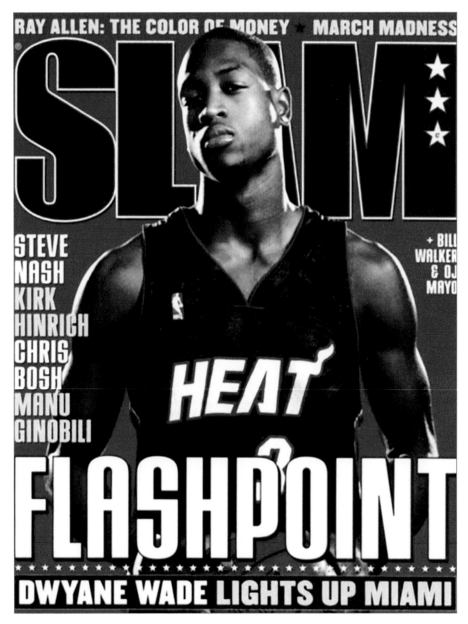

RAY ALLEN: THE COLOR OF MONEY ★ MARCH MADNESS

SLAM

STEVE NASH KIRK HINRICH CHRIS BOSH MANU GINOBILI

+ BILL WALKER & OJ MAYO

HEAT

FLASHPOINT

DWYANE WADE LIGHTS UP MIAMI

The cover of this May 2005 issue of *Slam* magazine had it right: Dwyane Wade was indeed lighting up Miami during his sophomore season. Dwyane finished the regular season averaging 24.1 points per game, 11th highest in the league. His 6.8 assists per game tied for 10th best in the NBA.

Afterward, Washington coach Eddie Jordan told sportswriter Reid how hard it had been to stop Dwyane when he was attacking the basket:

> **"You can't just stop him with one or two guys when he starts his power drives. He's quick, he's powerful, he's explosive and he's strong. That combination, all in a half-second, is deadly."**

⟫ THE STREAK ENDS ⟪

After being so hot in the first two rounds of the playoffs, Dwyane cooled off in Game One of the Eastern Conference Finals against the Detroit Pistons. He made just 7 of 25 shots and was held to 16 points as Detroit won, 90-81. He quickly bounced back with a 40-point, 8-rebound performance in Game Two, which Miami won, 92-86. A rib injury in Game Five sidelined Dwyane, but the Heat still won to take a 3-2 lead. Without Dwyane, the Heat were **routed** in Game Six, 91-66.

In spite of being hampered with the rib injury, Dwyane played in the decisive Game Seven. He did everything he could to help his team. He scored a game-high 20 points and had 4 assists, but Detroit won, 88-82.

Despite their disappointment, Heat fans felt they had a lot to look forward to in 2005–06. But Pat Riley wasn't willing to take future success for granted. He traded off four players and brought in others to replace them. There was also a rumor that the team roster wasn't the only thing that would change. Word was that Riley would replace Van Gundy as Miami's head coach.

⟫ A ROUGH START ⟪

Because of a sprained ankle, Shaq missed 18 of the Heat's first 21 games. Dwyane was playing well, but his team wasn't. Miami was 11-10—a winning record, but Heat fans were expecting a lot more from a team that was supposed to contend for a championship.

In December 2005, the Heat quickly called a press conference to announce that Pat Riley would replace Stan Van Gundy as Miami's head coach. Van Gundy said he was resigning so he could spend more time with his family. But many fans and sportswriters believed Riley wanted him to leave.

Riley had previously coached the Heat from 1995 to 2003. Although he had never won an NBA championship with Miami,

CROSS-CURRENTS

In 2005–06, Dwyane was voted to his second All-Star Game. For information about this event, read "The All-Star Game." Go to page 53. ▶▶

he had won four titles when he coached the Los Angeles Lakers from 1981 to 1990. During that time, the Lakers also won the NBA's Pacific Division title nine times. Heat fans expected Riley would turn things around.

At around the same time that Riley took over as head coach, Shaq returned to the starting lineup. Miami finished with a 41-20 spurt, giving them a season record of 52-30 and first place in the Southeast Division. They would start the playoffs against the Chicago Bulls.

⇒ A PESKY OPPONENT ⇐

Chicago's 41-41 record had earned them a tie for third place in the NBA's Central Division. That was just enough to get them into the playoffs. They might have been a lightly regarded opponent. Still, they were a proud and determined team, and gave Miami a tough opening-round series.

In Game One, Chicago was leading in the fourth quarter before Dwyane came through with six straight points. That gave the Heat a lead that they held for the rest of the game. Miami won, 111-106. Both Dwyane and Shaq posted double-doubles. Shaq had 27 points and 16 rebounds, and Dwyane had 30 points and 11 assists.

With the series tied at 2-2, Dwyane sustained a bruised hip late in the second quarter of Game Five. Fortunately, he was able to return to the game with 5:50 left in the third quarter. Miami was trailing, 55-50, but Dwyane's return sparked a 16-6 run, and the Heat led the rest of the way. Miami won easily, 92-78.

Shaq was the star of the series-clinching Game Six. He scored 30 points and grabbed 20 rebounds. Dwyane added 23 points and 6 assists in a 113-96 win for the Heat. Dwyane was delighted to be moving on to the next round, but there was no time to celebrate. If Miami was going to go all the way, it would have to play three more rounds.

⇒ NETS ARE NEXT ⇐

The New Jersey Nets got into postseason play by winning the Atlantic Division of the Eastern Conference. They advanced to face Miami by beating the Indiana Pacers, four games to two. They were not intimidated by Dwyane, Shaq, or anyone else on Miami's roster. The

Detroit Pistons guard Rip Hamilton contests a Dwyane Wade shot during Game Four of the Eastern Conference Finals, played at Miami's American Airlines Arena on May 29, 2006. Dwyane scored a game-high 31 points to pace Miami to an 89-78 victory, which gave the Heat a three-games-to-one series lead.

first game of the Eastern Conference Semifinals was a convincing win for the Nets. New Jersey jumped off to a 17-point lead in the first quarter and Miami never caught up to them while losing, 100-88.

DWYANE WADE

The Game One loss was a wake-up call for the Heat. Miami won the next four games to eliminate the Nets. Game Five saw Dwyane making a key defensive play that preserved Miami's 106-105 win. The Nets were one point down with one second left when guard Jason Kidd inbounded the ball. Dwyane correctly guessed where the ball was going and he broke for it, intercepted the inbounds pass, and held the ball till the buzzer sounded. Afterwards, he told *Sports Illustrated*'s Chris Ballard that all he wanted to do was break up the play:

In action from the 2006 NBA Eastern Conference Finals, Dwyane makes an acrobatic move over the 6'9" Antonio McDyess, whose Detroit Pistons teammates can only watch. Miami finished off the Pistons in six games to advance to the NBA Finals. Dwyane averaged 27.6 points and 6.6 assists per game—both tops among all players—in the series against Detroit.

“With one second left, all you want to do is make it tough. And I was able to get there, get my hand on the ball, and that was all she wrote.”

⇒ EASTERN CONFERENCE FINALS ⇐

If the Heat were going to move on to the finals, they would have to beat the team that ended their playoff run one year earlier—the Detroit Pistons. During the regular season, Detroit had posted the best record in the NBA (64-18). In the first two rounds of the playoffs, they had defeated Milwaukee and Cleveland. Even though Miami had won six of its last seven playoff games, most fans thought the Pistons were the better team.

For much of Game One, Shaq and Dwyane were in foul trouble. Still, Dwyane scored 25 points, and the Heat took a 91-86 victory. After Detroit evened the score by winning Game Two, Miami won Games Three and Four, before falling to Detroit, 91-78, in Game Five.

On the morning of Game Six, Dwyane drove himself to a hospital. He was sick with the flu and was feeling weak and **dehydrated**. At the start of the game, he still wasn't feeling well. He started off by missing four of his five shots and making three turnovers. Thanks to Shaq, Miami maintained control of the game.

When Dwyane returned early in the third quarter, the Heat were leading by 12. Dwyane closed out the quarter by scoring 10 points in nine minutes. Miami cruised to a 95-78 win and a trip to the NBA Finals.

⇒ WE ARE THE CHAMPIONS ⇐

Basketball will always be a team sport. No one player can do it all, but in the 2006 NBA Finals, Dwyane came close. While leading the Heat to the NBA championship over Dallas, four games to two, Dwyane averaged 34.7 points, 7.8 rebounds, and 3.8 assists. During the season, Coach Riley had come up with a team motto—"Fifteen Strong." It referred to the 15 players on Miami's roster. Instead of selfishly taking credit for leading the team, Dwyane said that the Heat won because they were a team of 15 who never quit believing in each other:

“That's what makes it sweet, because not at one moment did one of us not believe in each other. No matter what, in the locker room it was 15 strong.”

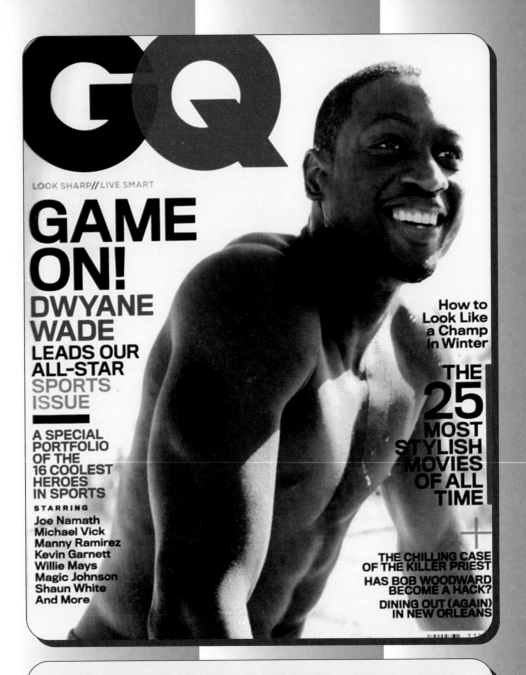

GQ

LOOK SHARP // LIVE SMART

GAME ON!
DWYANE WADE
LEADS OUR ALL-STAR SPORTS ISSUE

A SPECIAL PORTFOLIO OF THE 16 COOLEST HEROES IN SPORTS

STARRING

Joe Namath
Michael Vick
Manny Ramirez
Kevin Garnett
Willie Mays
Magic Johnson
Shaun White
And More

How to Look Like a Champ In Winter

THE 25 MOST STYLISH MOVIES OF ALL TIME

+

THE CHILLING CASE OF THE KILLER PRIEST
HAS BOB WOODWARD BECOME A HACK?
DINING OUT (AGAIN) IN NEW ORLEANS

Dwyane Wade was featured on the cover of the November 2006 issue of *GQ*. Inside, the men's lifestyle magazine profiled the 24-year-old basketball superstar and reigning NBA Finals MVP. Dwyane confessed to *GQ* writer Joel Lovell that he occasionally surprises himself during a basketball game. "Sometimes I'll do things on the court and be like, Wow, where did that come from?" Dwyane said.

5

Ups and Downs

SHORTLY AFTER WINNING THE 2006 NBA TITLE, the Heat rewarded their young star. Dwyane signed a three-year contract extension with an estimated value of $63 million. The extension meant that Dwyane would remain a member of the Miami Heat through 2010, with an option for 2011. It also made him one of the NBA's best-paid players.

Some media experts who follow the NBA were surprised that the Heat didn't try to sign Dwyane to a longer contract. It had been widely reported that a five-year deal might be in the works. But Dwyane was happy to be able to remain with the Heat. After signing the contract extension, he told the Associated Press that he was pleased he would be playing in Miami for several more seasons, at least:

> **"I got an opportunity once again to sign back with the Heat, the team that drafted me, and I'm looking**

forward to a bright future. I'm going to continue with the Heat as long as they want me. **" "**

⇒ INJURIES AND MISSED GAMES ⇐

When Dwyane was signed to a multiyear contract, Heat fans, sportswriters, broadcasters, and various pro basketball experts were all expecting the Heat to go deep into the playoffs in 2007. Coach Riley, Shaq, and all the key players from the 2006 championship team were going to be returning. Miami looked as if it might even win back-to-back championships. But injuries to Dwyane and Shaq, on top of an unexpected medical leave for Coach Riley, stalled the Heat's drive to another championship.

Coach Riley was the first to be out of action. In early January 2007, he took a leave of absence from coaching to undergo hip and knee surgery. During his absence, assistant coach Ron Rothstein stepped in to lead the team. Rothstein had been Miami's head coach during their first three seasons (1989–91). Under Rothstein, the Heat went 13-9, which kept them atop the Southeast Division.

CROSS-CURRENTS

To learn more about the Heat coach and president who had exerted a strong influence on Dwyane's career, read "Pat Riley." Go to page 54. ▶▶

Then Shaq dropped out of the picture when a cartilage tear in his knee made him miss 39 games. When he resumed playing in February, the Heat won six of their next seven games. Miami was making a strong push for the playoffs, but about three weeks after Shaq returned, they lost Dwyane. A shoulder injury took Dwyane out for 23 games. When he returned to the lineup, there were only six games left in the season.

With Dwyane out, but with Shaq and Coach Riley back, the Heat made a late-season surge. In March, they went 11-4 and Riley was named the NBA's Coach of the Month. The Heat finished the year with a 44-38 record—good enough to win the Southeast Division for the third straight year. Despite being on the injured list for six weeks and missing 31 games, Dwyane led the Heat in points scored, assists, and steals. He also led the Heat in scoring average, posting 27.4 points per game.

⇒ FOUR-GAME SWEEP ⇐

The Heat would defend their championship by facing the Chicago Bulls in the first round of the playoffs. Chicago had finished behind

Detroit and Cleveland in the Central Division of the Eastern Conference. If the regular season was any indication, Miami would have tough time getting by the Bulls. Prior to the playoffs, Chicago had beaten Miami in seven of their last eight encounters. In their season opener, the Bulls had routed the Heat, 108-66.

Dwyane watches from the lane as Chicago Bulls center Ben Wallace rises up for a slam dunk during Game Three of the first round of the 2007 NBA Eastern Conference playoffs. Chicago won the game, 104-96, and stunned the defending champion Miami Heat by sweeping the series, four games to none.

Dwyane had a good series against the Bulls. He averaged 23.5 points per game and had a double-double in Game Four. Yet, that wasn't enough to keep Chicago from sweeping Miami, 4-0. Heat fans were stunned by their team's early exit. For the first time in 50 years, the NBA's defending champions were swept in the opening round of the playoffs. After the Heat were eliminated, Dwyane didn't offer any alibis or excuses for their poor showing. He told Tim Reynolds of the Associated Press:

> **They were the better team. They won. We're not into what they were doing last year, saying they should have won. . . . They beat us fair and square. There are no ifs, ands or buts about it.**

REUNITED WITH HIS MOTHER

In spite of a disappointing season in 2007, Dwyane still had much to be thankful for. One thing was his ongoing relationship with his mother. Jolinda had gotten out of prison in 2003 and was no longer using drugs. She had become an **ordained minister**. Dwyane helped his mother get her life back on track by buying her a house and a car. He explained to *Jet* magazine that he wanted his mother to enjoy some of the things she had never had before:

> **It was always my dream to get my mother a house. She never lived in one, so I got her a nice house. . . . My mother never really drove before so she wanted to get her license. . . . She wanted to learn how to drive, so I helped teach her and bought her a car.**

OTHER GOOD WORKS

Dwyane's mother hasn't been the only person to benefit from his generosity. Dwyane is one of the few NBA players to donate 10 percent of his **pretax salary** to the church of his choice. It's a practice known as tithing. Dwyane tithes to the Blood, Water, and Spirit Ministry, a Baptist church in Chicago.

Dwyane also established the Wade's World Foundation in 2003. The foundation lends assistance to community-based organizations that support education, health, and social skills for at-risk children.

Dwyane speaks at a 2007 promotional event to launch his Wade 2.0 line of apparel and sneakers, made by Converse. His mother, Jolinda, is wearing sunglasses and holding a basketball. After many years as a drug addict and fugitive from the law, Jolinda Wade straightened out her life and reconciled with her family.

Among the organizations that receive financial support from the Wade's World Foundation are the Miami Children's Hospital, the Overtown Youth Center, and two churches.

Dwyane has also planned to someday build a youth center in the area of Chicago where he grew up. He credits his mother for inspiring him to start a foundation for helping the less fortunate. On his website, www.dwyanewade.com, he writes:

> **I can't just let basketball define who I am and what I am supposed to become. Like my mother always tells me, '[My life] is bigger than basketball.'**

Each year, Dwyane hosts a free summer basketball camp for almost 600 kids in Robbins, Illinois. This is just one of his many charitable endeavors. His Wade's World Foundation is dedicated to supporting at-risk children. "I can't just let basketball define who I am and what I am supposed to become," Dwyane has said.

⧽ ENDORSEMENTS ⧼

The Heat's playoff success in recent years greatly increased Dwyane's popularity and name recognition. His number 3 Heat jersey became the league's best-selling jersey for nearly two years. He began appearing on talk shows, and a number of companies hired him to endorse their products.

Dwyane has become so popular and well known that he even has some products that are named after him. His newest line of shoes with Converse—which he helped design—is known as the Wade 2.0. T-Mobile has released a series of Sidekick phones called the D-Wade.

The Internet search engine Google.com has been working with him to link the hundreds of

CROSS-CURRENTS

For more about how Dwyane has become one of the highest-paid young athletes today, check out "Product Endorsements." Go to page 55. ▶▶

Dwyane Wade basketball videos on Google and YouTube directly to Dwyane's website. Before long, Dwyane's income from endorsing products will exceed his already considerable income from playing basketball. In a recent magazine article, writer Roger O. Crockett explained why Dwyane has become so popular as a celebrity endorser:

> **"What brand managers love about Wade is his wholesome appeal. . . . Wade is a soft-spoken family man who married his high school sweetheart. He's not covered with tattoos. Modest and low-key, he's hip without the aura of urban menace."**

A still from a television commercial Dwyane Wade filmed for G2, a new low-calorie sports drink made by Gatorade. The commercial first aired on February 15, 2008, during coverage of the NBA Rookie Challenge, part of the league's annual All-Star Weekend. The 2008 All-Star Weekend was held in New Orleans, Louisiana.

⇒ A BAD SEASON ⇐

While things have been going well for Dwyane off the court, 2007–08 was a difficult season for him and the Heat. Miami started off by losing all seven of their preseason games. Once the regular season began, things didn't get much better. At the end of December 2007, the Heat were 8-23, and one month later, they had picked up only a single win and were 9-36. In February, they traded Shaquille O'Neal to the Phoenix Suns. But no matter what roster moves they made, the Heat kept losing. Following a 15-game losing streak, Dwyane expressed his feelings to Associated Press writer Tim Reynolds:

Entering the 2008–09 season—his sixth in the NBA—Dwyane Wade had staked his claim to being one of the premier players in the game. If Dwyane can avoid the kind of injuries that sidelined him for much of the 2006–07 and 2007–08 seasons, he may well carve out a career that leads to Springfield, Massachusetts, and the Basketball Hall of Fame.

❝I'm a competitor. Are there times when I want to come out and explode? Yes. But what is that going to do? What will that do for your team, in the locker room? I won't call anybody out because I have bad games and miss shots too. So I'm just focused on us turning this around, somehow.❞

⇒ MORE LOSSES ⇐

After the Heat's record fell to 11-50 in early March, it was announced that Dwyane would be sitting out the last 21 games of the season. That made him the third Heat player to be out for the rest of the season due to injuries. Center Alonzo Mourning and forward Dorell Wright were already out for the season with knee injuries. When the dust cleared on the disastrous 2007–08 season, the Heat finished with a league-worst record of 15-67—which also equaled the team-worst mark set by the Heat in their first year, back in 1988–89.

At the end of the 2007–08 season, Dwyane and the Heat decided that he would undergo OssaTron treatment. This high-tech therapy would send electric shock waves through his injured knee. The treatments are painful, but they have worked on other athletes.

Whatever the short-term results of this procedure might be, Dwyane has shown that he is one to rise above injury and pain. In May 2007, he had knee and shoulder surgery. At that time, doctors told him it would take a year before his knee would feel normal again. Still, Dwyane returned to play when he was in pain, and he was fifth in the NBA in scoring (with an average of 24.6 points per game) before going on the injured list in 2008.

⇒ THE FUTURE ⇐

As Dwayne recovers from his latest treatment, his fans are hoping the Heat can re-create the successes they enjoyed a short time ago. Because of their league-worst record in 2008, Miami received a high pick in the 2009 NBA draft. The young player drafted will probably help provide a foundation on which to rebuild for the future. But most people agree that the Heat's success will hinge on how well Dwayne returns from his injuries. His remarkable talent—both as a player and a leader—is irreplaceable.

NBA Expansion

A giant poster outside American Airlines Arena in Miami celebrates the 2006 Miami Heat team. The NBA added four expansion teams in the late 1980s: the Miami Heat, Charlotte Hornets, Minnesota Timberwolves, and Orlando Magic. Although the Magic reached the NBA Finals in 1995, the Heat became the first of the expansion franchises to break through and win an NBA championship.

During the 1980s, the NBA's popularity grew thanks to the emergence of several star players. Larry Bird of the Boston Celtics and Magic Johnson of the Los Angeles Lakers led their teams to multiple championships between 1980 and 1989, while Michael Jordan emerged as the league's most exciting young star during the mid-1980s. Other young NBA stars like Karl Malone and Charles Barkley joined established stars such as Julius "Dr. J" Erving and Kareem Abdul-Jabbar.

The on-court exploits of these big-name stars created a huge new fan base for the NBA. The league decided to cash in on its increasing popularity by adding four new teams: the Miami Heat and Charlotte Hornets in 1988, and the Orlando Magic and Minnesota Timberwolves in 1989.

In the Heat's first season, 1988–89, the team posted a dismal 15-67 record. By 1992, however, Miami had improved enough to advance to the playoffs for the first time. Between 1993 and 2005, the Heat reached the playoffs nine more times. Miami made it to the Eastern Conference Finals twice in that span, but they never made it to the NBA Finals. It was not until 2006, when the Heat beat the Detroit Pistons in the Eastern Conference Finals, that the franchise received its first chance to play for the NBA championship.

(Go back to page 6.)

NBA Finals MVPs

In 2006, Dwyane Wade became the first Miami player to win the Finals MVP Award. The trophy was first awarded in 1969. Even though the Celtics won the NBA title that year, the award went to a player on the losing team— Jerry West of the Lakers. Since then, a member of the championship team has always won the MVP Award.

Eight players have won the award more than once. During his fantastic career, Michael Jordan won it a record six times. Jordan also holds the record for highest scoring average by a Finals MVP. In 1993, Jordan set a record by averaging 41.0 points a game in the NBA Finals. He also averaged 8.5 rebounds and 6.5 assists per game that year to lead the Chicago Bulls to their third-straight NBA title.

Other repeat winners include Tim Duncan, Shaquille O'Neal, and Magic Johnson (three times each) and Kareem Abdul-Jabbar, Larry Bird, Hakeem Olajuwon, and Willis Reed (two times each).

In 1994 Olajuwon became the first player born outside the United States to win the MVP. Olajuwon was born in Nigeria. Tim Duncan, born in the U.S. Virgin Islands, became the second winner born outside the United States. And in 2007, Duncan's San Antonio teammate,

Tim Duncan of the San Antonio Spurs holds the NBA Finals MVP Award. Duncan, named MVP in 1999, 2003, and 2005, is one of eight players to win the award more than once. The others are Michael Jordan, Shaquille O'Neal, Magic Johnson, Kareem Abdul-Jabbar, Larry Bird, Hakeem Olajuwon, and Willis Reed.

Tony Parker, became the first European-born player to win the award. Parker was born in Belgium and raised in France.

(Go back to page 9.)

Dwyane's Role Model: Michael Jordan

The first time Michael Jordan led the Chicago Bulls to an NBA championship, in 1991, Dwyane Wade was nine years old. Dwyane has said that Jordan was his greatest role model as an athlete.

A combination of exceptional talent and personal charm made Jordan the most popular and widely recognized athlete of his time. After leading North Carolina to the 1982 NCAA title and starring on the gold-medal-winning U.S. team at the 1984 Olympics, Jordan began his NBA career. He won the league's Rookie of the Year Award in 1985—the first of many honors and awards he would receive.

All-Everything

Throughout his pro career, Jordan fascinated fans with his speed and gravity-defying leaping ability. He was the NBA's leading scorer 10 times, a league record, and ended his career with 32,292 points, the third-highest total in NBA history. Jordan was also an excellent defensive player, being named to the league's All-Defensive Team nine times. He was the league's Most Valuable Player five times.

He led the Chicago Bulls to NBA titles in 1991, 1992, 1993, 1996, 1997, and 1998. These two remarkable "three-peats" (1991–1993 and 1996–1998) were interrupted by the first of

Michael Jordan soars high during a slam dunk competition, which the NBA holds each year as part of its All-Star Weekend events. Growing up in the Chicago area, Dwyane Wade idolized the Chicago Bulls great, who led his team to six NBA championships in the 1990s.

what would turn out to be three occasions when Jordan retired from basketball.

Coming Back for More

Following the Bulls' first three-peat, and just before the 1993–94 season, Jordan said that he had lost his enthusiasm for basketball and decided to retire from the game. Not long afterward, Jordan announced his desire to play professional baseball and signed a contract with the Chicago White Sox. Following an unspectacular stint in the minor leagues, Jordan decided to return to the Bulls in the middle of the 1994–95 season and helped them make the playoffs. Although the team was eliminated from the 1995 Eastern Conference playoffs, Jordan and the Bulls dominated basketball for the next three seasons, which culminated in Chicago's claim to its second "three-peat" string of NBA championships in 1998.

Jordan retired for the second time in 1999, but he came back to the NBA in January 2000 as a part owner of the Washington Wizards and returned as a player for the Wizards in 2001. He retired for good in 2003. Today, Jordan is widely considered one of the greatest players in NBA history.

(Go back to page 12.)

History of the NCAA Tournament

The NCAA Tournament—today known as "March Madness"—had a fairly modest beginning. Only eight schools competed in the first tournament, held in 1939. The championship game drew an audience of 5,500. They saw Oregon beat Ohio State, 46-33. Today, millions of viewers watch worldwide, and sponsors pay hundreds of millions of dollars to broadcast their commercials during NCAA Tournament games.

In 1953, the tournament expanded to 22 teams. In 1954, the championship game was broadcast on television for the first time. The 1979 championship game between Michigan State and Indiana State remains the most-watched college basketball game of all time. Interest in the game was very high because the teams featured two very highly touted players—Indiana State's Larry Bird and Michigan State's Magic Johnson. Both would have Hall of Fame pro careers.

Before Dwyane led Marquette to the 2003 Final Four, the Golden Eagles had gone 26 years without advancing to the last round. In 1977, Al McGuire coached Marquette to its first and only NCAA championship when it defeated North Carolina, 67-59.

As the viewing audience has increased, the number of schools participating has expanded and the income generated by the tournament has grown. In 1985, the field expanded to its current 65 teams. In 2002, CBS agreed to pay $6 billion for the rights to broadcast all the games over television, radio, and the Internet for the next 11 years.

(Go back to page 15.)

The 2003 NBA Draft

Many people consider the 2003 NBA draft one of the strongest drafts of all time. Three first-round picks that year—LeBron James, Carmelo Anthony, and Dwyane Wade—have become superstars in the NBA.

With the first pick in the draft, the Cleveland Cavaliers chose LeBron James, a high school superstar from nearby Akron, Ohio. As expected, LeBron made a quick impact on his team. The Cavs improved from a 17-65 record in 2002–03 to 35-47 in LeBron's rookie season. In his fourth season, LeBron led the Cavs all the way to the NBA Finals.

The Denver Nuggets selected third in 2003, picking Carmelo Anthony. After posting the same 17-65 record in 2002–03 as the Cavaliers, Denver improved to 43-39 in Carmelo's rookie year. The Nuggets have reached the playoffs every season since Anthony joined the team.

Dwyane was the fifth player chosen in the first round of the 2003 draft. At the time, some scouts and basketball analysts thought the Heat had not made a good pick. ESPN writer Chad Ford called Miami's selection a "big shocker." Since then, however, Dwyane has proven that he can

Three of the first five players selected in the 2003 NBA draft, seen here in Team USA uniforms. From left: Carmelo Anthony, LeBron James, Dwyane Wade. James, the first overall pick, was drafted out of high school. Anthony, drafted third, had led Syracuse University to the NCAA national title in his freshman season. Miami's selection of Dwyane with the fifth pick surprised some basketball observers.

excel in the NBA. He's also helped his team win an NBA championship—something LeBron and Carmelo have yet to do. (Go back to page 17.) ◀◀

U.S. Teams in Olympic Basketball

In 1936, after successfully protesting a rule banning players taller than 6'3", the United States took the first gold medal in Olympic basketball by winning all four of its games.

The 1936 wins began the longest winning streak in Olympic basketball history. The United States won 62 games in a row and seven gold medals before being upset by the Soviet Union, 51-50, in 1972. The Soviets won when a hotly disputed decision added two seconds to the clock with only one second left in the game. The additional seconds gave the Soviets enough time to score a buzzer-beating, game-winning basket. In protest, the U.S. team skipped the awards ceremony and refused to accept the silver medal for their second-place finish.

The United States came back to win the gold again in 1976, but since then Yugoslavia, Argentina, and the Soviet Union have won gold. After a disappointing third-place finish in 1988, NBA players were allowed to compete. That led to the formation of what's been regarded as the greatest team in Olympic basketball competition.

The 1992 "Dream Team," led by superstars Michael Jordan, Larry Bird, Magic Johnson, and Charles Barkley, won all of its eight games by an average of 43.8 points each. U.S. teams also won the gold in 1996 and 2000 before falling to a third-place finish in 2004. (Go back to page 23.) ◀◀

The "Dream Team" of NBA stars that represented the United States at the 1992 Summer Olympics in Barcelona, Spain, did much to increase the popularity of basketball worldwide. The team beat its opponents by an average of 44 points per game en route to the gold medal. Seen here at the medals ceremony are (from left) Scottie Pippen, Michael Jordan, and Clyde Drexler.

Shaquille O'Neal

When Shaquille O'Neal was born, his mother gave him the name Shaquille Rashan, which is Arabic for "little warrior." Since then, Shaq has been a basketball warrior, but there's nothing little about him or his accomplishments.

After an outstanding high school basketball career, Shaq attended Louisiana State University.

At 7'1" and 325 pounds, Shaquille O'Neal has always been a force under the basket. Going into the 2008–09 season, Shaq was averaging 25.2 points and 11.5 rebounds per game over his 17-year NBA career. He won three NBA championships with the Los Angeles Lakers—garnering Finals MVP honors all three times— and he picked up another championship with the Miami Heat.

In his three years there, Shaq averaged 21.6 points and 13.5 rebounds a game—despite frequently being double- or triple-teamed. He skipped his senior year at LSU to enter the NBA draft and was the first player chosen in 1992.

Shaq made an immediate impact on his new team, the Orlando Magic. He became the first player ever to be named Player of the Week during his first week in the NBA. Shaq later joined the Los Angeles Lakers as a **free agent** and helped lead them to three straight NBA championships (2000– 2002). The big man was also the NBA's Champion- ship Finals MVP for all three of those years. In 2004, the Lakers traded Shaq to Miami for three players and a future draft pick. The trade helped Miami win its first NBA championship just two years later.

As he's gotten older, Shaq does not score or rebound as much as he once did, but at 7'1" and 325 pounds, he remains one of the league's most dominant players. In Feb- ruary 2008, Miami traded Shaq to the Phoenix Suns. (Go back to page 28.) ◄◄

The All-Star Game

Players are chosen to be in the NBA's All-Star Game in two ways. The first is by a vote of the fans. The leading vote-getters at each position in each of the league's two conferences (East and West) get to be the starters. The head coaches of the teams in each conference choose the rest of the squads. The only condition is that the coaches cannot vote for players on their own teams.

The All-Star Game came about because the NBA was looking for a way to increase attendance and fan interest. When the first All-Star Game was played in 1951, the league didn't have a television contract and some teams were struggling to stay in business. Major League Baseball had played a midseason All-Star Game since 1933, and the NBA decided to follow this example.

Today, the All-Star Game has become the centerpiece of a three-day event. Other contests held around the same time include a Slam Dunk Contest, a Three-Point Shootout competition, and a Skills Challenge in which players complete an obstacle course that tests their dribbling, shooting, and passing skills. (Dwyane won this event in 2006 and 2007.)

The 2008 NBA All-Star Game attracted a record worldwide television audience. The game, played in New Orleans, was broadcast in 215 countries and in 44 languages.

(Go back to page 32.)

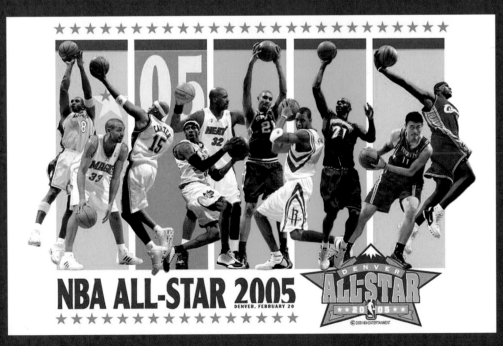

Dwyane Wade is fourth from right in this poster for the NBA's 2005 All-Star Game, held February 20 in Denver. Dwyane scored 14 points in 23 minutes. MVP Allen Iverson (fourth from left) dropped 15 points, and Vince Carter (third from left) added 11 to pace the East to a 125-115 victory.

Pat Riley

Pat Riley grew up in an athletic family. His father, Leon, was a major league outfielder for the Philadelphia Phillies. A brother, Lee, played professional football from 1955 to 1962. A gifted athlete himself, Riley was recruited by the University of Alabama to play football and by the University of Kentucky to play basketball. He chose basketball over football, and since then basketball has largely been his life.

After leaving Kentucky, Riley had had a nine-year career in the NBA. He played on the NBA champion 1972 Lakers, who are regarded as one the greatest teams in the history of pro basketball. During their championship season, the Lakers set a league record by winning 33 games in a row.

A Standout Coaching Career

But everything Riley accomplished as a player has been overshadowed by a coaching career in which he has won practically every coaching award that the NBA has to offer. In 24 seasons as an NBA coach, Riley has won five championships,

Miami Heat head coach Pat Riley hugs Dwyane Wade after the Heat's victory in the NBA Finals, June 20, 2006. Riley, who played in the NBA from 1967 to 1976, went on to become one of the league's most successful coaches. He guided the Los Angeles Lakers to four NBA championships before coaching the Heat to its title.

eight conference championships, and 17 divisional championships. He's won the NBA Coach of the Year Award three times while coaching three different teams—the Los Angeles Lakers, the New York Knicks, and the Miami Heat. In 1997, media members who cover the NBA named him one of the Top 10 coaches in NBA history.

A Difficult Time

Since December 2005, Riley has served as both the president and the head coach on the Miami Heat. He has had some very high highs and very low lows since taking on the two jobs. In 2006, the Heat won the NBA championship, but they were swept in the first round of the playoffs the following year. Then, in 2007–08, the Heat matched the club's worst record—15-67—previously set in 1988–89, their first year in the NBA. Miami had been hurt by injuries all season, but Riley refused to offer that as an excuse. He took the blame for their dismal season and continued to work hard at improving the team for the future:

"The buck stopped with me when we won the championship, and it stops with me right now when we've got the worst team in the league. I've got to try to rectify this and turn it around as soon as possible."

(Go back to page 38.)

Product Endorsements

Along with being one of the top players in the NBA, Dwyane is among the world's top athletes in another category—income from endorsing products. An **endorsement** is a public statement—usually by a celebrity or other high-profile person—that he or she approves of a particular product. Companies use advertisements featuring celebrity endorsements to get ordinary people to buy their products.

According to a November 28, 2007, article in *Fortune* magazine, Dwyane is ranked tenth among athletes in terms of endorsement income. Golfer Tiger Woods is the leader with an estimated 2007 income of $100 million in endorsement deals. LeBron James has the third-highest endorsement income overall and the highest among basketball players with $25 million. Others in the top 10 include Phil Mickelson ($47 million), Dale Earnhardt Jr. ($20 million), Michelle Wie ($19.5 million), Kobe Bryant ($16 million), Jeff Gordon ($15 million), Shaquille O'Neal ($15 million), and Peyton Manning ($13 million).

Dwyane became an attractive pitchman after the Heat won the 2006 NBA championship. In 2007, his estimated endorsement income was $12 million, thanks to deals with Gatorade, Converse, Staples, T-Mobile, the automaker Lincoln, and Topps Sports Cards.

(Go back to page 42.)

1982   Dwyane Wade is born on January 17 in Chicago, Illinois.

1990   After his parents divorce, Dwyane goes to live with his father, Dwyane Sr.

1992   Dwyane's mother, Jolinda, is arrested for possession of crack cocaine.

1996   Begins attending H. L. Richards High School in Oak Lawn, Illinois.

2000   During his senior year at Richards High School, Dwyane leads the basketball team to a 24-5 record while averaging 27 points and 11 rebounds a game.

2001   Accepts a basketball scholarship to attend Marquette University but has to sit out freshman year due to low test scores.

2002   During his first year playing at Marquette, leads team in scoring, rebounding, assists, steals, and blocked shots; marries his high school girlfriend, Siohvaughn Funches; first child, son Zaire, is born.

2003   Leads Marquette to a 27-6 record and a Final Four appearance in the NCAA Tournament; drafted by the Miami Heat in the first round of the NBA Draft; Dwyane's mother, Jolinda, is released from prison; she later becomes an ordained minister.

2004   Sets Miami Heat rookie record for scoring average; plays in his first NBA All-Star Game; Heat make the playoffs for first time in three years; Dwayne finishes third in Rookie of the Year voting in strong field behind LeBron James and Carmelo Anthony; plays on the U.S. Olympic team, which wins a bronze medal at the Summer Olympics in Athens, Greece.

2005   Heat post best record in the Eastern Conference, 59-23; Wade selected to start for the East in the All-Star Game; Miami starts playoffs with eight straight wins; they sweep Chicago and New Jersey before losing to the Detroit Pistons in the Eastern Conference Finals.

2006   Scores winning basket in the All-Star Game; Heat win their first NBA title by beating the Dallas Mavericks in six games; Dwyane is named MVP of NBA Finals; plays on U.S. team that wins a bronze medal at the 2006 FIBA World Championships in Japan.

2007   Heat make playoffs for fourth straight year, but are swept by the Chicago Bulls in four games; despite missing 31 games, Dwyane has his highest scoring average as a pro (27.4); chosen to play for the U.S. team at 2008 Summer Olympics in Beijing, China; second son, Zion, is born.

2008   Knee injury forces Wade to miss last 21 games of the season; Heat finish with worst record in NBA (15-67) and equal the worst record in franchise history, failing to make the playoffs for the first time since 2003.

2002   Named to All-Conference USA first team.
Honorable mention All-American Team.

2003   Conference USA Player of the Year.
Conference USA Defensive Player of the Year.
First team All-American.
MVP of the Midwest Regional in the NCAA Men's Basketball Tournament.

2004   Unanimous selection for NBA All-Rookie First Team.
Member of U.S. Olympic Basketball Team
Eastern Conference Player of the Month for December.

2005   Makes list of *People* magazine's 50 Most Beautiful People.
NBA All-Defensive Second Team.
East Squad, NBA All-Star Game.
All-NBA Second Team.

2006   East Squad, NBA All-Star Game.
All-NBA Second Team.
NBA Finals MVP.
Sports Illustrated Sportsman of the Year.
Skills Challenge Champion at NBA All-Star Game.

2007   Starts for East Squad in NBA All-Star Game.
All-NBA Third Team.
Skills Challenge Champion at NBA All-Star Game.

2008   Starts for East Squad in NBA All-Star Game.

Career NBA Statistics

Season	G	ppg	rpg	apg	spg
2003–04	61	16.2	4.0	4.5	1.4
2004–05	77	24.1	5.2	6.8	1.6
2005–06	75	27.2	5.7	6.7	2.0
2006–07	51	27.4	4.7	7.5	2.1
2007–08	51	24.6	4.2	6.9	1.7

Key

G = games played
ppg = points per game
rpg = rebounds per game
apg = assists per game
spg = steals per game

Books

Finkel, John. *Future Stars of the NBA: Dwyane Wade, LeBron James, and Carmelo Anthony*. Los Angeles: Tokyopop Inc., 2005.

Savage, Jeff. *Dwyane Wade*. Minneapolis: Lerner Publications Co., 2007.

Smithwick, John. *Meet Dwayne Wade: Basketball's Rising Star*. New York: PowerKids Press, 2007.

Stewart, Mark, and Matt Zeysing. *The Miami Heat*. Chicago: Norwood House Press, 2006.

Young, Jeff C. *Burning up the Court: The Miami Heat*. Berkeley Heights, N. J.: Enslow Publishers, Inc., 2008.

Web Sites

www.dwyanewade.com

Dwyane Wade's official Web site offers the latest news about him along with photos, videos, wallpapers, message boards, and news about his charitable foundation.

www.Heat.com

Miami Heat fans can find all the latest news about their favorite team. The site also has links to the team's history, recent magazine and newspaper articles about the Heat, photos, videos, and a message board. Heat fans can also download wallpaper of Dwyane Wade and other Heat players on this Web site.

www.nba.com

The official Web site of the National Basketball Association. Fans can get all the latest scores, stats, and news and link to the Web site of their favorite NBA team. Video highlights of selected games are also available.

www.usabasketball.com

The official Web site of the U.S. Men's and Women's Basketball National Teams that will compete at the 2008 Summer Olympics as well as other international competitions. Visitors to the site can find a biography of Dwyane and all the other players.

http://sports.espn.go.com/nba/allstargame

ESPN's 2008 All-Star Game site features links to latest news and developments in the NBA plus features on all the players and angles in the 2008 All-Star Game. Of special interest: an audio feature on Dwyane Wade that includes an interview.

aura—a distinctive quality that characterizes a person or thing.

catalyst—a person or thing that brings about an event or change.

dehydrated—not having enough water in the body.

double-double—an individual performance in which a player has double-digit numbers in two of the following categories: points, rebounds, assists, steals, or blocked shots.

double-team—to use two players to guard one player.

endorsement—an ad or commercial for a product or service, done in return for money or other compensation.

free agent—an athlete who is not under contract to a team and is free to sell his or her services to the highest bidder.

initiate—to begin or originate.

motion offense—a plan that uses player movement to take advantage of the offensive team's quickness.

ordained minister—a person who has been authorized by a church to lead and conduct religious services.

point guard—the guard who runs the team's offense by controlling the ball.

precocious—characterized by unusually early development, skill, or intelligence.

pretax salary—a person's salary or pay before taxes are deducted.

rectify—to remedy or correct.

routed—defeated overwhelmingly.

shooting guard—the guard who has the main duty of scoring points for his or her team.

triple-double—an individual performance in which a player has double-digit numbers in three of the following categories: points, rebounds, assists, steals, or blocked shots.

triple-team—to use three players to guard one player.

page 6 "Thirteen points down . . ." S. L. Price, "Sportsman of the Year: Dwyane Wade," *Sports Illustrated* (December 11, 2006), p. 23.

page 8 "I'm just in rhythm . . ." "Wade, Heat Overwhelm Mavs to Even NBA Finals," http://www.nba.com/games/20060615/DALMIA/recap.html.

page 9 "We tried a lot of things . . ." NBA.com, "Postgame Quotes." www.nba.com/mavericks/matchup/postgame_quotes_062066.html.

page 9 "This is a team award . . ." InsideHoops.com, "NBA Trophy Presentation Transcript." http://www.insidehoops.com/trophy-presentation-062206.shtml.

page 12 "[My father] taught me the game . . ." Dan Firrincili, "Dwyane Wade," *Current Biography Yearbook 2006* (New York: H.W. Wilson, 2006), p. 571.

page 18 "God has blessed me . . ." Price, "Sportsman of the Year: Dwyane Wade," p. 23.

page 20 "At the beginning . . ." Ian Thomsen, "Heat Seeker: Thanks to Rookie Dwyane Wade, Miami Is Back in the Playoff Hunt," *Sports Illustrated* (March 8, 2004), p. 83.

page 22 "No rookie, including LeBron . . ." Ian Thomsen, "Heat Seeker," p. 83.

page 25 "I wasn't excited to get . . ." Sean Deveney, "Wade's mission: forget Athens," *The Sporting News* (November 1, 2004), p. 56.

page 25 "From junior high on up . . ." Brett Ballantini, "A steal of a deal," *Basketball Digest* (November/December 2004). http://findarticles.com/p/articles/mi_m0FCJ/is_1_32/ai_n6332441.

page 27 "Believe it. The emergence of . . ." Jack McCallum, "Super Sidekick: In just his second season, versatile guard Dwyane Wade (a.k.a. Flash) has turned Miami into the team to beat," *Sports Illustrated* (January 17, 2005), p. 58.

page 28 "Wade controlled the game . . ." Eric Reid, "Red Zone Diaries: The Wonder of Wade," Heat.com. http://www.nba.com/heat/multi-media/redzone_diaries_050512.html.

page 31 "You can't just stop him . . ." Reid, "The Wonder of Wade."

page 35 "With one second left . . ." Chris Ballard, "It Was All in a Night's Work," *Sports Illustrated Presents Miami Heat Special Collector's Edition* (July 5, 2006), p. 39.

page 35 "That's what makes it sweet . . ." NBA.com, "Wade Leads Heat to First NBA Championship." www.nba.com/games/20060620/MIDAL/recap.html.

page 37 "I got an opportunity . . ." Associated Press, "As expected, Wade signs shorter contract with Heat." ESPN360.com (July 13, 2006). http://sports.espn.go.com/nba/news/story?id=2516735.

page 40 "They were the better team . . ." Tim Reynolds, "Bulls sweep Miami out of NBA playoffs" (April 29, 2007). www.panatagraph.com/articles/2007/04/29/sportsextra/doc46350f38c1206662801722.txt.

page 40 "It was always my dream . . ." Clarence Waldron, et al., "Showing their love: celebs reveal the first gifts they've given mom." *Jet* (May 14, 2007), p. 19.

page 41 "I can't just let basketball . . ." Wade's World Foundation. http://www.dwyanewade.com/fans/foundation.php

page 43 "What brand managers love . . ." Roger O. Crockett, "Building a Megabrand Named Dwyane," *Business Week* (February 12, 2007), p. 82.

page 45 "I'm a competitor . . ." Tim Reynolds, "The Rise and Fall of the Miami Heat," North Port (Fl.) *Sun-Herald* (January 26, 2008), p. S5.

page 55 "The buck stopped with me . . ." Associated Press, "Riley might miss games to scout NCAA talent." NBC Sports (March 6, 2008). http://nbcsports.com/id/23504939/.

Numbers in ***bold italics*** refer to captions.

Jeff C. Young lives in North Port, Florida, and is a graduate of Ball State University. He has written over twenty-five books for young readers. His book *Bleeding Kansas and the Violent Clash Over Slavery in the Heartland* won the 2007 Spur Award from the Western Writers of America for Best Juvenile Nonfiction Book.

PICTURE CREDITS

page

1: David Sherman/NBAE/Getty Images

4: Ronald Martinez/Getty Images

7: Glenn James/NBAE/Getty Images

8: C.W. Griffin/Miami Herald/KRT

10: ASP Library

13: Converse/NMI

14: Marquette University/PRMS

16: Topps/NMI

19: Victor Baldizon/NBAE/Getty Images

21: Issac Baldizon/NBAE/Getty Images

23: Miami Herald/KRT

24: Nestle/NMI

26: Converse/PRMS

29: Issac Baldizon/NBAE/Getty Images

30: Slam/NMI

33: Brian Bahr/Getty Images

34: Victor Baldizon/NBAE/Getty Images

36: GQ/NMI

39: Eliot J. Schechter/Getty Images

41: Converse/PRMS

42: Wade's World Foundation/PRMS

43: Gatorade/NMI

44: NBA/CSMG Sports

46: T&T/IOA Photos

47: NBAE/Getty Images

48: NBA/SPCS

50: Nathaniel S. Butler/NBAE/Getty Images

51: Mike Powell/Getty Images

52: NBAE/SPCS

53: NBA/NMI

54: Ronald Martinez/Getty Images

Front cover: NBA/CSMG Sports